FROM THE PINE
OBSERVATORY

FROM THE PINE
OBSERVATORY

George Messo

halfacro**W**n

h a l f a c r o W n

First published in Great Britain in 2000
by halfacrown publishers
198 Victoria Avenue
Kingston upon Hull HU5 3DY

Printed in Great Britain by
Copytech UK, Peterborough

ISBN 0 9537022 3 5

Acknowledgments

Some of these poems have appeared or are due to appear in the following magazines: *Envoi, The European Anthology, Intimacy, The Journal of Contemporary Anglo-Scandinavian Poetry, Lines Review, Megrim, Oasis Magazine, Outposts, Pearl* (USA), *Pennine Platform* and *The Rialto*.

'Prose from the City of Trees' first appeared as a Markings pamphlet, *No. 14* (Cloud, 1996). 'Eclogues' was printed in *Three poems of Giuseppe Ungaretti* (Plague Press, 1996). Twelve of these poems were published in an Oasis Books pamphlet, *In a Station House* (1997).

The publishers would like to express their thanks to Peter Didsbury for his invaluable editorial help in the production of this volume.

I was about to plunge into a reflection on imprisoned birds,
when I was disturbed by noise and the laughter of children
ASBJØRNSEN

CONTENTS

I

Crossroads, Nearing Carver

The brother and she sit in silence,
with no particular place to go,
happy driving new roads into parlance.

She's reading a book by Unamuno
called *La agonia del cristianismo*.

It's autumn. They've not said a word
for months. If the egg in her throat
should crack they'd be lost. Yet they'd
gladly drive forever in this arcane
triangle of the low alluvial plain.

He stops the car and smiles. I reckon,
any minute now, something will happen.

Three Notes

It's in the wood-pile
wind exacts a tongue,
hollows the sap-pool.

(The hedge winy with dew
demonstrates the *logos* of a field system,
a calculus of place-ends and possession.)

Bearing low over limestone strata:
winged demi-gods of the swarthy marsh,
their ululant to spear and stop the heart.

Prose from the City of Trees

I INCOGNITO

There was, to begin, the ontology of its
tap. Found in a strange nub of the city: a
fallen cane.

Echoes down drainage shafts, angst born
of wood bridges.

In its owners mind the halo of a street
lamp vanishes.

II INSIDE THE ANTIQUE SHOP NOTHING STIRS

Between going and making still. A child
hovers among paving cracks, ankles
lighter than balloons, knowing there are
doors and windows the rain entreats in
voices not its own.

Gathered to inspect phenomenal
obsequies, we scatter at footfalls.
Passing away, in spite of them, as if to
increase the incidence of wonder. To
upend an idling orrery. Fattened by such
licks of sweetness.

III DISQUIET

And how should we have known, had
the clown's facial tic been a sign
pointing to the boatless river?

Through green verbs of the shimmering
birdhouse - those bough-lipped
natterings - we travelled by tram, sure of
its inevitable transports.

When finally we disembarked, propelled
from the shifting carriage, we were
skaters gliding over thin ice at the lake's
hem. Clusters of dark souls gathered
beneath us. Faces, of those we had left
behind, pressed to the underside of its
vast, intractable surface: gaping and
godforebound.

Epistolary Matters

Today it's water he loves.
An unmentionable flick on arcs beneath bridges,

Parkside weirs given up to brilliance,
Or, "An opining drip's endless patience."

Quill in hand, with poised loquacity,
Father Bob sends word to the vestry.

- If we read: his politics are the unimpaired
Locutions of mute sensa bristling to be heard. -

Perched on his ecumenical bidet,
He writes to say: it's water he loves today.

Eclogues
from the Italian of Giuseppe Ungaretti

I QUIET

The grapes are ripe and the field ploughed,

The mountain wears a halo of clouds.

On summer's dusty mirrors
A shadow has fallen,

Between uncertain fingers
The light is sure,
Far-reaching.

With the swallows goes
The last anxiety.

II AGONY

To die like a gasping lark
seen through a mirage

Or like a quail
who has lost
the will to fly
and dies marooned
by an arm of the sea

But not to live lamenting
like an eyeless finch.

III VIGIL

Throughout the night
lying beside
a slaughtered
comrade
his mouth
curled out
grinning at the full moon
his stiffened
hands
reaching
into my silence
I've written
letters full of love

Never have
life and I
been so close.

Waterfall with Rowan

Notice first
the water-veins
edging into dark,

a cooling cup
where shadows
drink up shade.

Above the din
an iridescent lip
is sucked of light

and gravity floods in.
Endlessly unrepeated.
A witching wrist

the flashing trees
give vibrancy -
its piercing fruits

blood-shot eyes
of wildcats
hanging.

In a Station House

Racks of smoke from an iron gullet.
I think it's fair to say, though do correct me,
The signalman is nesting a fuelled spark in the coke stove.

Old forms of ungoverned semblance rise and curl
What hands they touch us with. Quoff
And whoop through an untenanted loft.
Frisk the tiled roof like a flute, and off.

But held this long afternoon by lingering fog.
An indigestible weirdness lodged in the river's tidal mouth,
As if our very souls were what it fed on.

And beyond the breachable embankment:
Low bass pules of a siren's rarefied
Squall echo a preternatural portent,
Signal our passage on the outgoing tide.

Panegyric

A cataract cooks
on the yolky eye
exactly shelled
of an eggshape
cupped from its crowns.

All head & neck
dim chick-yack
cannonades
gone memory
knows only where.

No wingsome
thrash no
globe-bound
thrall no
centrifugal cack.

Thing –
say, if it were –
now soul-deposed
and liquid skip:
a sizzling saltarello.

A Detail

Dusk is mooching by the claypit
In a low-field-scene from Jan van Loon,
Sipping light off a tile stowed pallet.

A ball of gnats spins its ovoid mass
To rafted, reed-spired latitudes.

In my insect allegory flies mimic
Words, shady forms the poets use
To score their dust of unfamiliar music.

II

Ode from a Hat

Night was falling and in the murky light
filtering through the narrow window the
hat with its flat rim and urn-like shape
assumed a strange significance. A
mysterious door swung on its hinge. Time
limped in. Outside a hitherto unheard-of
man span curious facts from wool: angora
barns, mohair cattle doors; improbable
rural scenes.

Life became something lodged in my throat
and though the hat was far too small for all
it must accommodate I opened doors to
unleash much wider voids: parameters
delibly etched in thorn, of the low plain
hammered down by skies, a greenness fully
succulent, wholly kempt.

Night was falling fast and in the gloom the
hat seemed to be growing larger. In the
great non-scheme-of-things particulars
were all I knew; the rusting soil-clogged
coulter rising, inches only, inches now, its
dip and comb just so; a sub-terrain of dyke
and drain; the known width of hedges.

Now the enormous hat sat there, rebuking them and
blocking the way with that single piece of paper lying inside
it which nobody was willing to take. Just when it seemed the
landscape's felt rim cocked to my skew-whiffed sense, the hat
itself finally disappeared through a trap-door in the text. I
knew then this misunderstanding with myself would prove
more subtle than *that.*

From the Pine Observatory

There is a man with coloured glass
erecting rainbows and a church
where stars drop in for candlemass.

His gavelled heart's a wooden block,
an ink's malign relief. He'll call it
"Water of Minnoch at Kirriereoch".

★

Post-rain in a peat-tinged burn
the salmon's metaled flanks
photo-flash a pool.

In woodland ghettos
autumn deals are done,
on cranking down and slowing up,

planting a brute full-stop to ground.
A leaf-walled sarcophagus
disputes these mindful realms,

strange to the rig's inanima,
whose waters sea-bound shunts
go busying through a glen.

Night-Moves

Ten holy nights -
even Tea
chants Namu Amida Butsu

BUSON (1715-83)

To evade
the gamekeeper,
I wade
a little deeper.

★

Bewitched
be whispers
of the flyfisher's
roll & switch.

★

Corona Borealis -
you might
say the night
was made of this.

Verlaine's Paranoiascope

I NIGHT AND SKY

Blue or black. Nulled
beside an empty field.
Vast and tender
and insistent like a river.

Briefly,
in a clearing of the copse,
an interjection of song:
a wren devouring the heads of insects.

II LUNAR

Chinese white
enlivens the woods;
to each wet briar
its own voice
below the bower...

The pond gathers
silhouettes
shades
of the dumb oak
where a wind tore...

III IN THE WOODS

1.   They find only pallid charms
       – innocent or lunatic – taken
       from woods warm-breezed

       and scented. While I, nervous
       and rawly paranoid, daub
       my canvas white as fury.

       Summer is the worst; its
       dissolution into grey dusk
       at once trivial and profound.

2.   A guinea-fowl rustles in the under-cut
       – my mind throngs with old wives' tales –
       like an assassin waiting to strike.

Seriously Duane, the Workshop

NEVER end a line with *love*.
It's the devil's dick to rhyme with it.
To *shove a foxglove up a dove*
Ask yourself: will the *love-glove* fit?

III

Mirror Me

Insouciant by five
the jug is dry.
Belly-up on blades
the lawn cuts lovingly
a cleft her head indents.
Heat is liquid too
as sober she
inspects a drunken me.
It's now we misconstrue
this need to reinvent
a morning's brief *ennui*,
tap the heart's tirades.
The jug held high
we drink ourselves alive.

More Epistolary Matters

Light caught by the old net-curtain
fills an angle of the room,
for a moment like a gothic minster.

Those fay conceits
digest my thoughts,
alert to lesser space.

Dear Jane, though I am brief,
in three days
I will have invented the postcard.

Field-Talk
for Peter and Pat

I

There is a poem by Pär Lagerkvist
which begins:
A kind of beauty is born at dusk.

For months this *kind of* puzzled me.
But *this* morning
Pär is reading aloud his poem. Listen

awhile to the increase
rapture will afford him:

The heavens dispense their love...
– Almost I am embarrassed
to hear him say that word *love* –

...which hovers a moment
over the fields,
over the house-strewn earth.

II

You gift us, Pär,
unimagined nothings.
Who am I to lance
that glassy cell at dawn,
your Swedish lyric pore
or stem the gawping whirl
of a life I'm falling through.
Maybe it's God,
you'll say, *obscures*
these far-off things.
– But is it, Pär,
the barley god,
a god of rippling wheat,
so fine and yet so faint?

III

At the edge of a field, at the edge of the world, dawn asphodels – who'd doubt them immanence? – ignite their perishable dew, (on a morning lik this, casually there) berate my numb self to elation.   A thousandt time scorch the field's hoary nerve   where crop heads swell to snuff the light.   I clock the pause and the poet, Lagerkvist, whose voice embalmed for us these deft colluding species, a time and place. So his poem is the last we shall ever hear, the mantric vowel of wind on leaf, a tree-hymn, that soft whoosh receding for eternity.

The Village, in Kafka

I

If I saw through gaps in the timorous foliage,
then fleetingly. Flash of sun-caught wheel
or voices summer-brimmed whose language

meant only joy. Farmhands were coming
from the fields, stooped and dark-imbued.
Their harvest wagons obscured everything.

II

Banks of carrion crows rose up, till
sky and land assumed a seamless visage.
Lights from the children's bikes were shrill
stars descending into our blackened village.

III

What if, even now, the unfathomable rising
air betrays us, the tyranny of a sense
we newly find is heard, to name something –

songs, like a red-hot poker in the mouth,
their drawn primordial scream pressing
out, making for some town in the south.

Adolf Paul on a Visit

Fear of ravens
      loose in her
            inhabits a room

your trembling hand
      augments.
            It's the corner

of Friedrichstrasse,
      That Oslo girl,
            opposite the Polish

pharmacy. To leer
      down snow-
            quartzed precincts

of a gaze,
      her wild-eyed
            darkness

peered upon.
      What black mass
            looms within

her parrots throat:
      villain of the thousand
            chamber scenes!

She does not look,
      he thinks, *much*
            like a saint at all.

Lick

At this point I forget
        stars too are on.
It will happen yet.
        – But when? – Soon

dusk's cool wave has
        lapped us. A radio
swings. Loose jazz
        oozes mellow-

ness. An eardrum
        opens to a highway
in another town some
        twenty years away.

At this point I forget
        cars too move on.
It will happen yet.
        – But when? – Soon

enough the heart's too full
        to house me.
Your automatic earful
        might otherwise be

jazz a radio swings,
        tunes that dispossess
undress the loving skin's
        loose mellowness.

At this point I forget.
        Cool licks prolong
a lover's epithet.
        soon it will be gone.

Four Corbieres

1. THE CABIN-BOY

Hey! So your old man's a salt?
– A fisherman, or was. He's dead.
One night he left my mother's bed
And sleeps in a shroud of cobalt...

In chapel there's a tomb she tends
– Though fuck all's there. –
Until her kids grow up she depends
On bread I earn: their welfare.

Two little brats. – *So, was anything found*
On the beach where your old man drowned?...
– His pipe-case and his clogs...

On Sundays mother cries herself to sleep.
– But I'll get my revenge for their upkeep
And make sailors of her sprogs!

2. LETTER FROM MEXICO

"You gave me charge of the lad. – Fish-bait!
And a few of his mates too, poor shits.
The crew... They're all fucked. We misfits,
        Maybe, will come through. – It's fate. –

"Nothing's as sweet as that – Sailor – for a man;
We've all got our sea-legs on land – for sure.
No puking there. No arse tilting to Orion.
        It's not the life of an epicure!

"As for me, old *shore-pal*, I'm in tears over this.
Without fear, I'd gladly have given my skin
To send him back to port... Me, I'm a ruin:
        You can't argue with delirium's kiss.

"The fever here's as sure as Lent in Spring.
We go to the grave-yard to draw our ration.
The Zouave – Parisian no less – is always saying
        It's a 'Garden of Acclimatisation'.

"Console yourself. They're dropping off here like flies.
... In his bag I found some things you'll recognise:
A picture of a girl, and a small transistor,
        And: marked – *Gift for my sister*. –

"He wanted his *Ma* to know: his prayers were said.
And *Pa*: that he'd rather have died like a man.
In his final hour angels sat beside his bed:
        A soldier. The other, a seaman."

3. EVIL LANDSCAPE

Dune of old bones. – Death-knells,
Wave wracked: crushing sound on sound...
– Pale marsh, where the moon dwells
Sucking worms on its nightly round.

– This plagued repose, where fever
Burns... The damned wisp languishes.
– Stinking grass where the sorcerer,
A yellow-bellied hare, vanishes.

– The white laundress unloads
The dead's foul linen
Before the *sun of wolves*... Those toads,

Tiny sad-singing-fools,
With their colics venin,
The mushrooms, their stools.

4. RONDEL

It's dark, child, thief of stars!
Night and day have closed like an oyster;
Sleep... let them come, petit bourgeois'
Who bleat: Never! And scoff: Forever!

Do you hear their clicking tongues?... Their
                            anal reservoirs?
Oh, those delicate vowels!... their polite ordeals...
It's dark, child, thief of stars!

Smell their sick perfumes... their *farts from the crypt.*
Sleep: and forget the tomb-reek of genteels;
Your glass-heart's a shrine and love's your postscript.
Sleep... let them come, those petit bourgeois'.
It's dark, child, thief of stars!

IV

Foregatherings

Every story has the same ending,
And every song is an old song.

Ibsen, Peer Gynt

I

A fogbank's mute cell.
Are pier bells struck
to fill their rivercomb.

Time translates a tide.
Soon my father
will load the space
I've left to write
the only poem
I'll ever place him in.
But what is place?
A river-bounded plain
that slips beyond
the endless eyescapes reach.
An estuary of mudflats
sounding off through marshy tracts
made perfect level fields.

And turning now
its girded inward arm
distils a sudden calm.

II

Unthinkable. To pierce
the husky ventricle

significance enfolds –
a field-drain's lambency

(whose meaning makes a sea)
sloops soundly in

to mince with it,
moil of the fleet estuary.

III

On far-out buoys
spume licked gulls
pit hideous shrieks ashore.

Soon, my father will load the space I've left.

He barely knows how not to be
relied on, however late you like.
Euphemistically, his "lost at sea"
is almost prescient, ghostlike.

IV

Vaguely seen
the semaphore he waves in.

Wave?

A porous sense some
voice would speak
foregathers into sound.

V

I saw him by the quay, with fish.
A wall-eyed arctic stare, not dead
but dreaming. Looking in.
The socket cupped, a mirror-ball
of glass-ice in the hold.

So, it is not too late to mourn,
through partial dark, a cataract
the drunken fish-eye lens will graze
to gaze at him, my father
dead beneath the waves.

VI

"I drifted with the tides   nosing out
    through silty dark   a whirl
once open   vanishes   voluminous
   sea   a flux too large to anchor
    moved with tides   on fins
and tailed   all winter-headed   deaf
to surge and spume   peninsulas
     no wave had held so tight
    day on endless day   I rolled
forever deep   beyond   the sleeping
  estuary   and home   a distant thing
   where green-sweet tastes   of sugar
    came and went   in there
my wine flowed rudder-cut   a wash
  of green on blue or blue on green
   as one   I drifted with the tides
    submerged in a prism of stars
devouring mirror-calm   voluminous
sea   no tocsin sounds the coastline
  now bemoans a blown cadaver's
    fatal dip   ecstatic wreck
    your briny salt-licked brow
  all blueness fat   and thoughtful
I drifted with the tides   and watched
  as lightening ripped apart the skies
watched as clouds of plankton rode
   on gulf-stream undertows   far
above   as dawn broke   their dream
  darkened sunlight   mystically so
    filtered through a violet haze
  a crashing wave was all it took

to set new scenes afloat
and the sea
rose with its own unshakable dream
grain-eyed   were froths   unknown
to me   where the rip's blown memory
writhed in phosphorescent arcs   turned
heads   hysterical herds   stampeding
reefs   in suicidal waves   unleashed
their snorting muzzled foams   one
deafening roar crashed shoreward
and I
swam   once more with jellied wrecks
no tocsin sound bemoans   of the
bloated lip's last speaking   waves
released their heavy breath   a taunting
hollow tone   crumbling from one own
exhaustible core   out   and out
in far-dissolving calms   horizons
discuss skies   my one embracing void
of blue on endless blue   quiescent
drawn to its own concluding quiet
I thought
of home   too far a place   my body
sick and slow   but blindly on   dissolving
with the tides   ungoing then   fin-
ally to stop
and think no more of home..."

Factish

That surf of wind-blown wheat
No stranger thing than this -
A whirling half-formed wave
His smoothened slate has skimmed.

Skyward drafts of heated ash
Are realms his embers ride.
A fire to warm himself. Some
Facts. A place he'll incarnate.

A Reed Cutter
for Madeleine

Gut pangs
shape an appetite.
From field to fence,
through gate and scrub

that skin on wood,
knock, handles now
a spoon as who
might hold a scythe?

★

Horizons
come and go,
lay undisturbed
on bodies rocked

by thoughts – who
dared to think them? -
fathers pass to sons.

★

A half-filled bowl
receives the lip
quivering, quelled,
the fingers tilt to it.

Each cheekful,
then, is dwelt -
how first a feeling
consecrates the thought.

What hungry look
the sated eyelids cut,
as slurp recedes to sip:
a licked rim glistening.

Weltschmerz

Stone, a vault you least admire.
One night you picked me up
Unthinking thing a rheumy heat

The sexed-out fingers traced.
Who knows what hands you have
Or where you place them now.

One night you picked me up,
Contorted spine, my edgy atom–
Vault, a stone you least admire.

Abandoned Village

From high rookeries
scurrilous imprecations
goad the sun to its charge.

Summoned up or roused in air
catalytic spores of warted fungi
steam from forest floors.

Whole lanes of vines
where the squat fruit clings
to its fatness. Soon their trembling

world is lichen bedded, branching out
to Hart's tongue ferns licked inky wet.
Demented bracken waving. Then,

as now, in abstract lines a fossil cusp
– some scaly past was lost to me –
comes hurling forward through the dark.